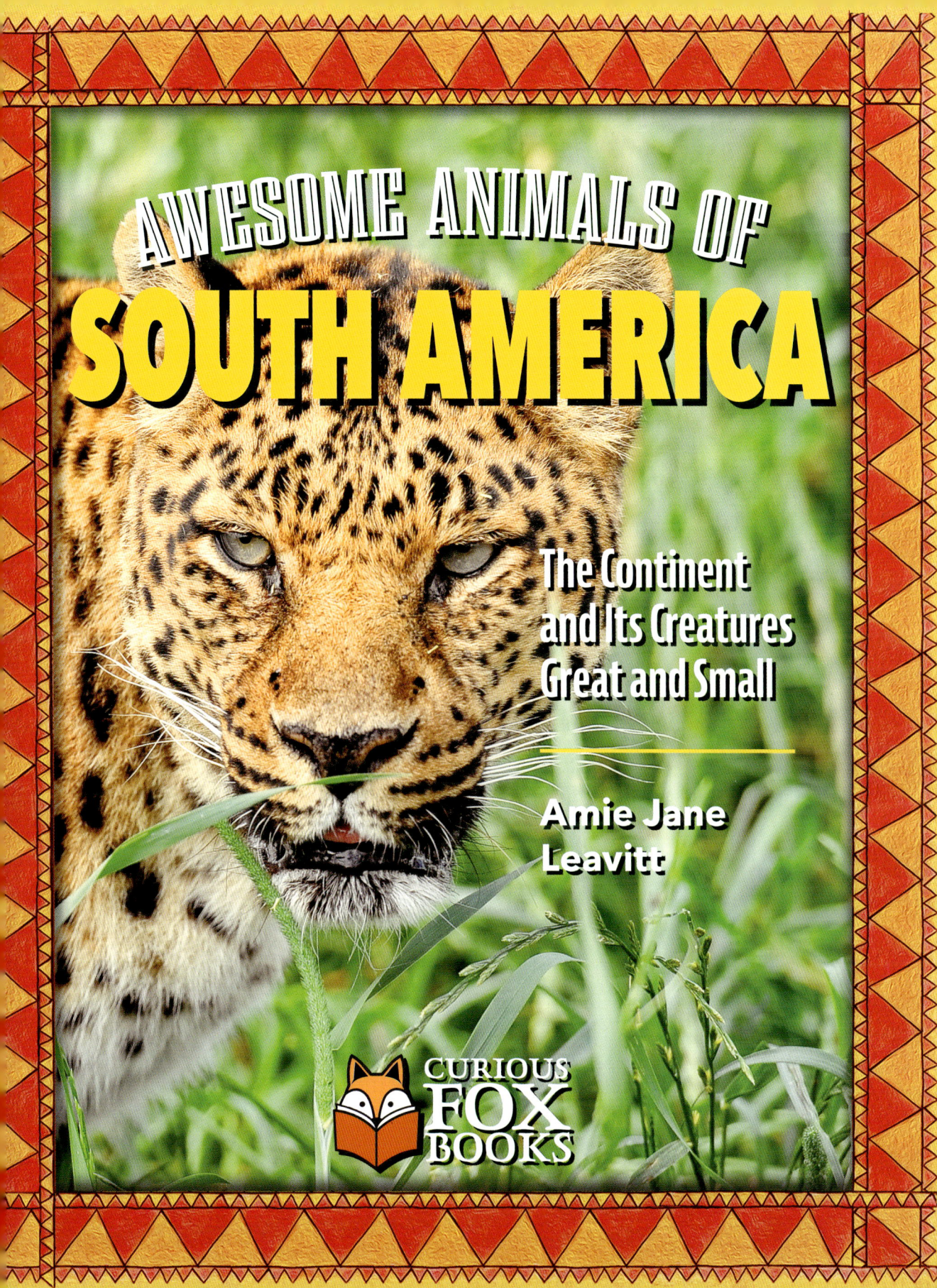

AWESOME ANIMALS OF SOUTH AMERICA

The Continent and Its Creatures Great and Small

Amie Jane Leavitt

CURIOUS FOX BOOKS

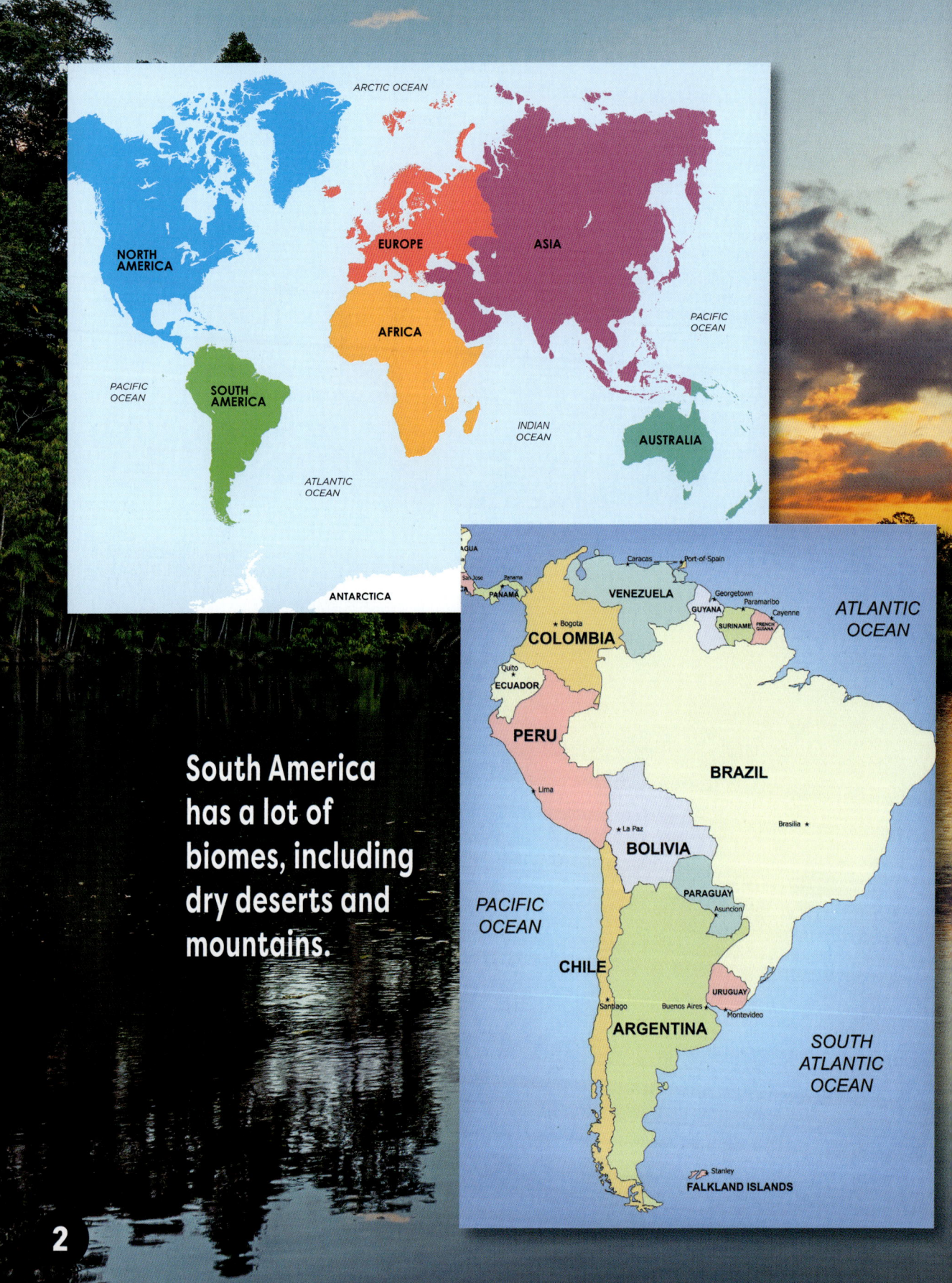

South America has a lot of biomes, including dry deserts and mountains.

2

Welcome to South America! This continent stretches from just above the equator all the way down near Antarctica. The Amazon River flows across the land to create the Amazon rainforest. It is home to millions of kinds of animals, including the piranha **(per-AH-nuh)** fish. Their teeth are similar to sharks' teeth.

RED-BELLIED PIRANHA

Length: 20 inches (51 centimeters)
Weight: 8½ pounds (3.9 kilograms)
Habitat: rivers and lakes of South America, especially the Amazon River
Diet: worms, insects, fish, fruits, and leaves

Meet the mighty jaguar, the largest cat of the Americas. Its jaws and teeth are strong enough to break the shell and thick skin of its prey. When a jaguar has an all-black coat, it is called a black panther.

JAGUAR
Length: 9 feet (2.7 meters), including tail
Weight: 250 pounds (121 kilograms)
Habitat: rainforests, swamps, grasslands, and deserts of northern and central South America
Diet: turtles, caimans, fish, and medium or large mammals

The Atacama (ah-tah-KAH-mah) Desert is in Chile (CHIL-ee). One part of the desert did not have any rain for 400 years! Still, there are lakes here. Flamingos live near these lakes. These birds have long, skinny legs and bright pink feathers. They get their pink coloring from the algae and shrimp that they eat.

ANDEAN FLAMINGO
Height: 4½ feet (1.4 meters)
Weight: 10½ pounds (4.8 kilograms)
Habitat: wetlands of Chile, Argentina, and Bolivia
Diet: fish, shrimp, algae, and aquatic plants

CHINCHILLA

Length: 11 inches (240 millimeters), not including tail
Weight: 28 ounces (794 grams)
Habitat: mountains of Chile, Peru, and Bolivia
Diet: grains, leaves, and cactuses

The chinchilla (**chin-CHIL-ah**) lives high up in the Andes (**AN-deez**) Mountains. Its thick, soft fur is great for keeping out the cold in the chinchilla's chilly habitat.

The southern viscacha (**vis-KAH-chuh**) is similar to a rabbit. It bounces from rock to rock in its mountain home.

SOUTHERN VISCACHA

Length: 16 inches (41 centimeters), not including tail
Weight: 6½ pounds (3 kilograms)
Habitat: mountains of Chile, Argentina, Peru, and Bolivia
Diet: grasses and mosses

Alpacas and llamas also live in the Andes. They look very similar, but alpacas are smaller than llamas. Llamas are used as pack animals, carrying things for people as they travel through the mountains.

Alpacas have very soft fur. They are sheared like sheep, and their fur is used to make clothes. Llamas have coarse fur that is sheared and used to make rugs and ropes.

ALPACA
Height: 3½ feet (1.1 meters)
Weight: 150 pounds (68 kilograms)
Habitat: mountains of Chile, Peru, Bolivia, and Ecuador
Diet: grasses

LLAMA

Length: 6 feet (1.8 meters)
Weight: 400 pounds (181 kilograms)
Habitat: mountains of Chile, Peru, Bolivia, and Ecuador
Diet: grasses

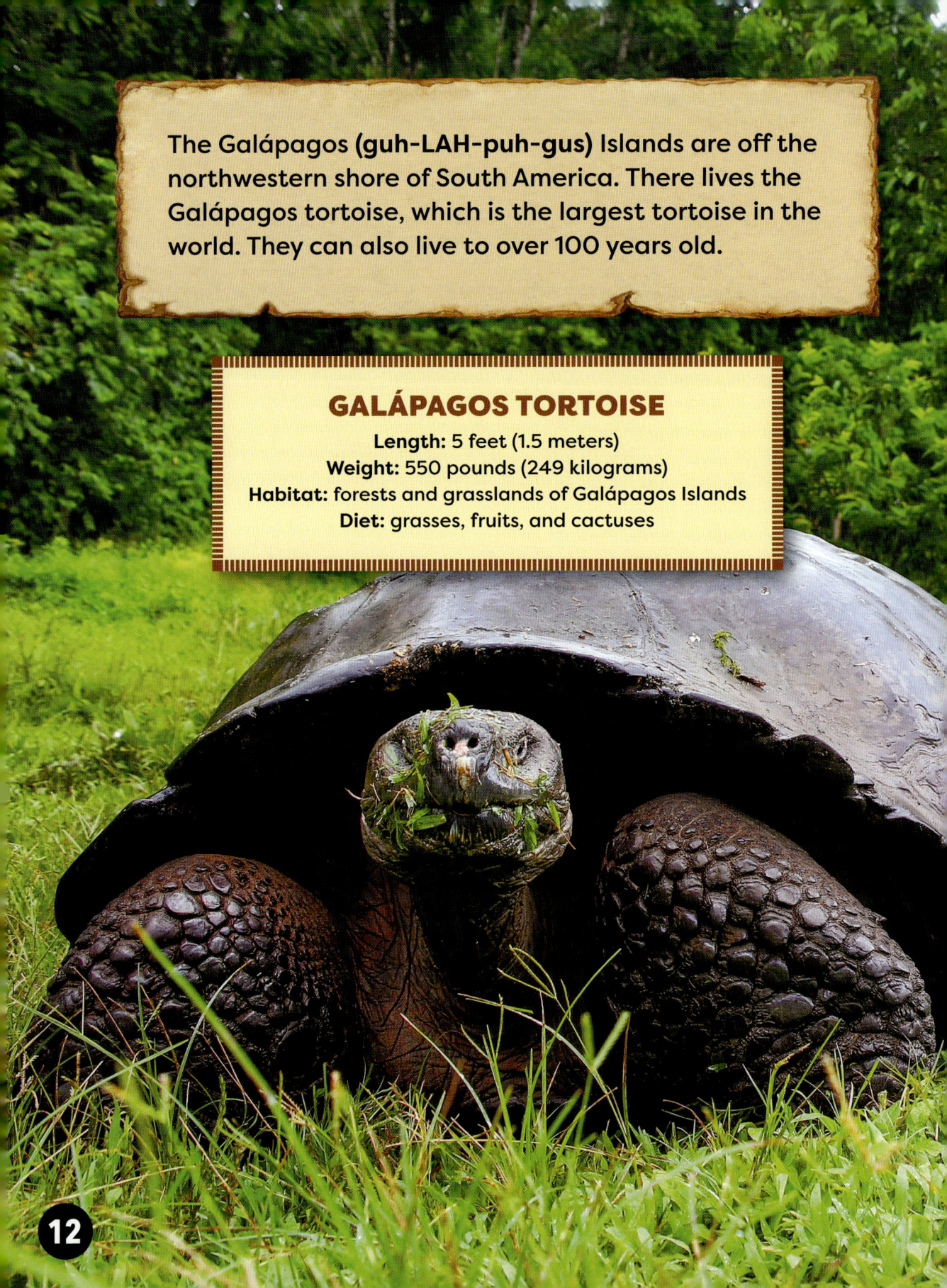

The Galápagos (guh-LAH-puh-gus) Islands are off the northwestern shore of South America. There lives the Galápagos tortoise, which is the largest tortoise in the world. They can also live to over 100 years old.

GALÁPAGOS TORTOISE
Length: 5 feet (1.5 meters)
Weight: 550 pounds (249 kilograms)
Habitat: forests and grasslands of Galápagos Islands
Diet: grasses, fruits, and cactuses

MARINE IGUANA

Length: 4 feet (1.2 meters), including tail
Weight: 28 pounds (13 kilograms)
Habitat: beaches and swamps of Galápagos Islands
Diet: algae

Marine iguanas are another unique animal found here. They are the only lizards that go into the ocean. These iguanas dive in the water for food to eat, and they can stay underwater for an hour.

Near the equator, most of the land in South America is a rainforest. This steamy jungle and its rivers are rich in animal life. Many of these animals are brightly colored.

The golden dart frog is poisonous. The imperial (im-PEER-ee-uhl) tortoise beetle hides its legs and head when it's attacked, just like a tortoise. The cockatoo cichlid (SIK-lid) are also a common sight in aquariums.

GOLDEN DART FROG

Length: 2 inches (5 centimeters)
Weight: 1 ounce (28 grams)
Habitat: rainforests of western Colombia
Diet: insects

COCKATOO CICHLID
Length: 3½ inches (8.9 centimeters)
Weight: 1 gram
Habitat: streams of the Amazon River
Diet: insects and worms

IMPERIAL TORTOISE BEETLE
Length: ½ inch (1.3 centimeters)
Habitat: rainforests of Brazil
Diet: leaves

GREEN ANACONDA
Length: 30 feet (9 meters)
Weight: 550 pounds (249 kilograms)
Habitat: rainforests of northern and central South America
Diet: deer, caimans, and jaguars

The green anaconda is the largest snake in the world. This snake does not poison its prey. Instead, it will squeeze, then it swallows the animal whole. The anaconda's dull green and brown colors help it hide in rainforest rivers.

KEEL-BILLED TOUCAN
Length: 22 inches (56 centimeters)
Weight: 18 ounces (510 grams)
Habitat: rainforests of Venezuela and Colombia
Diet: fruits, insects, eggs, and lizards

Toucans live in the forests of South America, including the Amazon rainforest. They are very colorful and have large beaks. The toucan's beak is about one third of its body length. It will tuck its beak under a wing when sleeping.

Another colorful bird found in the rainforest is the macaw. It has a strong beak to break open nuts for food. Macaws are great at imitating sounds, including human speech!

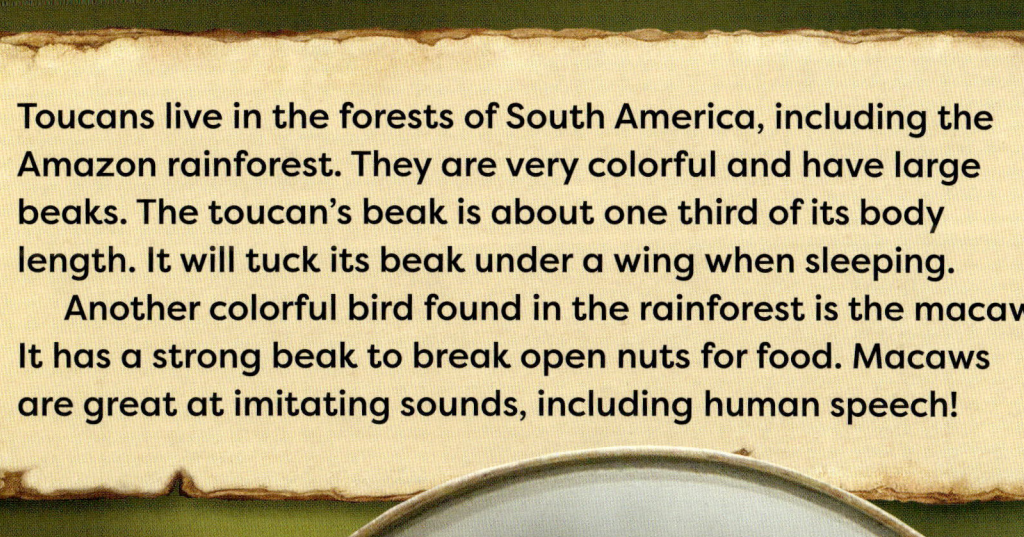

SCARLET MACAW

Length: 33 inches (84 centimeters)
Weight: 2 pounds (907 grams)
Habitat: forests of northern South America
Diet: nuts, seeds, berries, and leaves

Two-toed and three-toed sloths are the slowest-moving mammals on earth. They spend most of their life hanging from tree branches. Because they move slowly, sloths are harder to spot in the trees. Sloths stay so still that green algae will grow on their fur. The color also helps them hide from predators.

BROWN-THROATED SLOTH
Length: 27 inches (69 centimeters), including tail
Weight: 14 pounds (6.4 kilograms)
Habitat: rainforests of Brazil and northwestern South America
Diet: leaves and fruits

The capybara (cah-pih-BEAR-ah) is related to the guinea pig. But the "capy" is the world's largest rodent.
    Capys live near rivers and will swim regularly to find food. They have webbed feet to help them swim. The capybara will give rides to birds, which eat any bugs they find on its back.

CAPYBARA
Height: 2 feet (60 centimeters)
Weight: 174 pounds (79 kilograms)
Habitat: swamps, wetlands, and forests of northern and central South America
Diet: grasses, aquatic plants, and fruits

SOUTH AMERICAN TAPIR

Length: 6 feet (1.8 meters)
Weight: 600 pounds (272 kilograms)
Habitat: rainforests and wetlands of northern and central South America
Diet: leaves, aquatic plants, and fruits

The tapir (TAY-per) has a trunk like an elephant, but it is more closely related to the rhino. A tapir's trunk can be used as a snorkel when swimming.

Giant anteaters have a long tongue that is inserted into anthill or termite mounds. It can eat up to 30,000 insects in one day.

GIANT ANTEATER

Length: 8 feet (2.4 meters), including tail
Weight: 140 pounds (64 kilograms)
Habitat: forests, wetlands, and grasslands of northern and central South America
Diet: ants and termites

COATI

Length: 22 inches (56 centimeters), not including tail
Weight: 16 pounds (7.3 kilograms)
Habitat: forests and grasslands of northern and central South America
Diet: insects, lizards, and fruits

The coati (coh-WAH-tee) likes to live in trees, but it isn't a monkey. It is related to the raccoon and has a long, striped tail. Coatis have long noses that are handy for sniffing out food to eat on the ground or in trees. A group of coatis is called a band.

Related to the coati is the kinkajou (KINK-ah-joo). It has the nickname of honey bear because it likes to eat nectar and honey. The kinkajou has a 5 inch (12.7 centimeter) long tongue.

KINKAJOU
Length: 30 inches (76 centimeters), not including tail
Weight: 10 pounds (4.5 kilograms)
Habitat: forests of northern and eastern South America
Diet: fruits, nectar, and leaves

There are many kinds of monkeys in the rainforest. They can hang in the trees from their hands, feet, or tail. Tamarin (TAM-ahr-in) monkeys talk to each other by making calls, trills, and whines. The golden lion tamarin has a mane like a lion.

From the rainforests in the north to the deserts and frozen conditions in the south, many different types of animals call South America home.

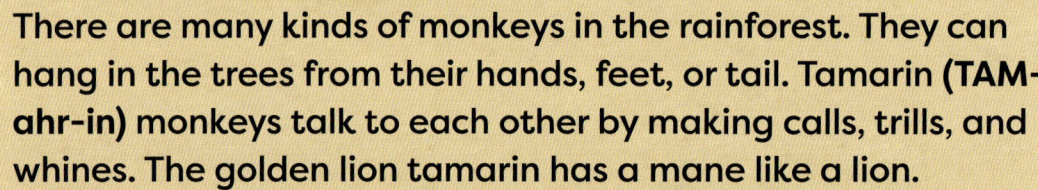

COTTON-TOP TAMARIN

Length: 8 inches (20 centimeters), not including tail
Weight: 1 pound (450 grams)
Habitat: forests of northwestern Colombia
Diet: fruits, nuts, insects, and eggs

FURTHER READING

Books

Aloian, Molly. *A Rainforest Habitat.* Washington, D. C.: National Geographic School Publishers, 2010.

Gibbs, Maddie. *Flamingos.* New York: Rosen PowerKids Press, 2011.

Gregory, Josh. *Sloths.* New York: Scholastic, 2015.

Lonely Planet Kids. *The Travel Book: A Journey Through Every Country in the World.* New York: Lonely Planet, 2015.

Perkins, Chloe. *Living in . . . Brazil.* New York: Simon Schuster, 2016.

Websites

Active Wild: South American Animals
https://www.activewild.com/south-american-animals

The San Diego Zoo: South America
https://animals.sandiegozoo.org/regions/south-america

National Geographic: 10 Amazing Amazon Facts!
https://www.natgeokids.com/uk/discover/geography/physical-geography/amazon-facts

GLOSSARY

algae (AL-jee)—Simple plants that do not have roots, stems, leaves, or flowers. They generally live in water, in large groups.

biome (BY-ohm)—Any major region that has a specific climate and supports specific animals and plants.

burrow (BUR-oh)—To dig a hole or tunnel in the ground.

caiman (CAY-men)—An animal related to alligators.

continent (KON-teh-nent)—One of the seven great pieces of land on Earth.

equator (ee-KWAY-ter)—The middle band of the Earth that is the same distance from both poles.

nectar (NEK-ter)—Liquid coming out of plants and flowers.

predator (PREH-deh-ter)— An animal that hunts other animals for food.

rainforest—Area where it rains daily.

PHOTO CREDITS

Inside front cover—Shutterstock/ruboart; p. 1—Tambako the Jaguar; p. 2 (world map)—Shutterstock/Maxger; p. 2 (continent map)—Shutterstock/Creative Jen Designs; pp. 2–3—Shutterstock/SL-Photography; p. 3 (piranha)—Shutterstock/Grigorii Pisotsckii; p. 4 (inset)—Shutterstock/AB Photographie; pp. 4–5—Charles J. Sharp; p. 6 (flamingo close up)—Shutterstock/Steve Allen; pp. 6–7—Carlos Urzuna; p. 8 (chinchilla)— Shutterstock/Anke Licht; pp. 8–9— Shutterstock/Wirestock Creators; p. 10 (alpaca)—Shutterstock/Shirelady; pp. 10–11—Shutterstock/Vladimir Melnik; pp. 12–13—Shutterstock/Don Mammoser; p. 13 (iguana)—Shutterstock/Kimberly Shavender; pp. 14–15—Shutterstock/Chanintorn.v; p. 15 (cichlid)—Shutterstock/ Andrzej Zabawski; p. 15 (beetle)—ASM Monteiro; pp. 16–17—Shutterstock/Vaclav Sebek; p. 17 (inset)— Shutterstock/Patrick K. Campbell; pp. 18–19 (all) Shutterstock/Ondrej Prosicky; p. 20 (inset)—Shutterstock/Ondrej Prosicky; pp. 20–21— Shutterstock/ Milan Zygmunt; p. 22 (inset)—Shutterstock/Ondrej Prosicky; pp. 22–23—Shutterstock/RicardoKuhl; pp. 24–25—Shutterstock/raymond orton; p. 25 (anteater)—Shutterstock/Luiz Kagiyama; pp. 26–27—Shutterstock/Christian Musat; p. 25 (kinkajou)—Shutterstock/Wim Hoek; p. 28 (golden lion tamarin)—Marie Hale; pp. 28–29— Shutterstock/Nagel Photography; inside back cover Shutterstock/ruboart.

All other photos—Public Domain. Every measure has been taken to find all copyright holders of material used in this book. In the event any mistakes or omissions have happened within, attempts to correct them will be made in future editions of the book.

CHECK OUT THE OTHER BOOKS IN THE AWESOME ANIMALS SERIES

Awesome Animals of Africa
Awesome Animals of Antarctica
Awesome Animals of Asia
Awesome Animals of Australia
Awesome Animals of Europe and the United Kingdom
Awesome Animals of North America

© 2024 by Curious Fox Books™, an imprint of Fox Chapel Publishing Company, Inc., 903 Square Street, Mount Joy, PA 17552.

Awesome Animals of South America is a revision of *The Animals of South America*, published in 2017 by Purple Toad Publishing, Inc. Reproduction of its contents is strictly prohibited without written permission from the rights holder.

Paperback ISBN 979-8-89094-111-4
Hardcover ISBN 979-8-89094-112-1

Library of Congress Control Number: 2024933156

To learn more about the other great books from Fox Chapel Publishing, or to find a retailer near you, call toll-free 800-457-9112 or visit us at *www.FoxChapelPublishing.com*.

We are always looking for talented authors. To submit an idea, please send a brief inquiry to acquisitions@foxchapelpublishing.com.

Fox Chapel Publishing makes every effort to use environmentally friendly paper for printing.

Printed in China

World Map

- **PACIFIC OCEAN**
- **ASIA**
- **AUSTRALIA**
- **ARCTIC OCEAN**
- **INDIAN OCEAN**
- **NORTH POLE**
- **GREENLAND**
- **EUROPE**
- **AFRICA**
- **ANTARCTICA**
- **SOUTH POLE**
- **ATLANTIC OCEAN**
- **NORTH AMERICA**
- **SOUTH AMERICA**
- **PACIFIC OCEAN**